LINCOLNWOOD PUBLIC LIBRARY

3 1242 00225 4044

W9-CCS-746

Lincolnwood Library
4000 W. Pratt Ave.
Lincolnwood, IL 60712

To each and every EXPERT—to those parents, grandparents, teachers, librarians, caregivers, child development specialists, pediatricians, nurses, child psychologists, and psychoanalysts who read over and looked over our work, talked to us, taught us, and corrected us over and over again as we created this book for young children. We could not have created this book without you. THANK YOU!—R. H. H.

For Shelley, Yvonne, Nola, and Margo
N. B. W.

Text copyright © 2012 by Bee Productions, Inc.
Illustrations copyright © 2012 by Nadine Bernard Westcott

All rights reserved. No part of this book may be reproduced, transmitted, or stored in an information retrieval system in any form or by any means, graphic, electronic, or mechanical, including photocopying, taping, and recording, without prior written permission from the publisher.

First edition 2012

Library of Congress Cataloging-in-Publication Data is available.

Library of Congress Catalog Card Number 2011046668

ISBN 978-0-7636-3631-9

12 13 14 15 16 17 TLF 10 9 8 7 6 5 4 3 2 1
Printed in Dongguan, Guangdong, China

This book was typeset in Berkeley Old Style.
The illustrations were created digitally.

Candlewick Press
99 Dover Street
Somerville, Massachusetts 02144

visit us at www.candlewick.com

ER
306.85
HAR

Who's In My Family?

All About Our Families

Robie H. Harris

illustrated by Nadine Bernard Westcott

CANDLEWICK PRESS

Wherever you live, wherever you go, there are all kinds of families.

Families live in so many different kinds of places.
In cities. In towns. In the countryside.
In apartments. In houses. Or on farms.
Families live near lakes. Near rivers. Near oceans.
In the desert. In the mountains. Or on grassy plains.

Families eat many different kinds of food for breakfast.
Some families eat bacon, eggs, bagels, and juice.

Some eat oranges, blueberry pancakes, and milk.

Some eat pita bread, hummus, cucumbers, and olives.

Some families eat soup, shrimp dumplings, and rice.

Some eat raspberries, bananas, granola, and yogurt.

Some eat papaya, burritos, and hot chocolate.

Families love to be together. Families go to the market, to the library, to the doctor, to the dentist, to the park, to the zoo—and to so many other places together.

Families fly kites, ride bikes, play catch, get haircuts,
buy new shoes, visit friends or grandparents—and do
so many other things together.

People families are one kind of family. There are also animal families—squirrel families, polar bear families, sea lion families, zebra families, giraffe families, hippopotamus families, tiger families, and so many other kinds of animal families.

Children are born into their families or adopted into their families. And most children live with and grow up in their families. Some families have one child. Some have two children.

Some families have three or four or more children. Some have twins. Some have triplets.

Look! The polar bear family has two bear cubs in it! I bet they're twins. What an AWESOME family!
My friend's family has three kids in it— TWINS and a BABY! What a COOL family!

Many families have grown-ups and children in them.
Some families have only grown-ups.

Some families have a mommy and a daddy. Some have a mommy. Some have a daddy. Some have two mommies. Some have two daddies.

Some children live with their mommy part of the time and with their daddy part of the time.

Some children live with their daddy and a stepparent. Some live with their mommy and a stepparent.

In some families, everybody's hair is the same—mostly wavy, or mostly curly, or mostly straight. In other families, people have different kinds and different colors of hair.

In some families, everybody has almost the same skin  color. In other families, people have different skin colors. In some families, people's eyes are different colors or different shapes. In other families, people have the same color eyes or the same shape eyes.

Sometimes a grandparent, or aunt, or uncle lives with a child's family. And some children live in their grandparent's, or aunt's, or uncle's, or foster parent's home.

Parents, sisters, brothers, grandparents, cousins, aunts, and uncles can all be part of a child's family. Often, good friends or a pet can be part of a child's family too.

Families have happy times together.

Sometimes, children get a runny nose, a sore throat, a fever, or a tummyache, or scrape a knee, or cut a finger, or just feel bad.

Families help their children feel better and get well.

If I get a tummyache, Mommy or Daddy holds me on their lap. And then I feel a lot better.

Parents and kids help each other clean up, put away toys, and feed their pets.

After supper, our puppy licks up EVERY crumb on the floor. Our puppy helps our family clean up!

Parents help their children take a bath, wash and dry their hair, brush their teeth, and get dressed for bed.

At nighttime, our family also reads stories together. Sometimes we read the same story three times in a row!

Every day and every night and all around the world, families talk, laugh, sing, play, cuddle up, tell stories, read books, and make sure their children are healthy and safe and loved.

Most of all, and most of the time, and no matter what—children and grown-ups and their families really do love one another!